Connecting Moments

Elevate your High Holiday Experience

Selected insights from:

Rabbi DovBer Pinson,

Rabbi Joseph Telushkin,

Rabbi Roly Matalon and

David Solomon

Edited by Mark Pearlman

SINAI LIVE BOOKS

Imprint of Rethink Partners, LLC

Copyright © 2012 by Rethink Partners, LLC

Rethink Partners books may be purchased for educational, business or sales promotional use. For more information please contact Rethink Partners, LLC at info@rethinkpartners.com.

ISBN-13: 978-0615661087 (Sinai Live Books)
ISBN-10: 0615661084

High Holiday Preparation

The High Holidays

From the Editor: Aha! Moments

Mark Pearlman

There is a mystical concept in Judaism that you are your name ("For as his name, so is he" [Samuel I:25; 25]). The name for this book series is Sinai Live, in reference to our experience at Mount Sinai when God revealed the Torah. Back then that was the "big Reveal" – with a capital R. Now our hope with the publication of these books is to offer teachings that reveal (with a small r, at least) how to make your personal journey more meaningful and connected.

Sometimes the right words at the right time can unlock the deepest insights. Sinai Live is about guiding you to these "Aha! Moments" – moments of clarity that stay with you forever. Through concise and thoughtful books, we hope to make Jewish wisdom relevant to our daily lives, ultimately guiding us to be better people and have better relationships with those around us and with God. We want to live up to our Sinai name.

To that end, this *Connecting Moments* book was published to help make the High Holiday time more meaningful. The book is an outgrowth of our collaboration with some of the world's top Rabbis and teachers, who over the years – on camera and at truly memorable events – have shared with us the secrets to transforming the High Holiday experience.

For the first edition of this book, we compiled a collection of interviews and essays to help you foster your own Aha! moments. We hope you experience a few, and that your High Holidays become a more meaningful experience because of them.

Read on and *L'Shana Tova*,

– Mark Pearlman

Creator of Rethink Partners Publishing & Sinai Live Books (connect@sinailive.com)

Introduction

Rabbi Roly Matalon

A learned individual once came to see the Kotzker Rebbe. The man, in his thirties, had never before been to a rebbe.

"What have you done all your life?" the master asked him.

"I have gone through the entire Talmud three times," the guest replied.

"And how much of the Talmud has gone through you?" Reb Mendl inquired.

We open the High Holy Days with *Selihot* (prayers of penitence) and in the span of two and a half weeks we will have gone through the *Yamim Noraim*. How much of the *Yamim Noraim* will go through us? Will they be just another High Holy Days or will we allow them to become a truly intense, creative, new and spontaneous spiritual adventure? Will we be uninhibited enough, authentic enough, daring enough to let an avalanche of emotions, feelings, memories, longings, prayers and insights flow in and out of our souls?

The Hebrew root for *shanah* (year), Sh N H, exists in a fascinating tension and perplexity. Indeed, Sh N H means at the very same time to change *and* to repeat and therefore the New Year invites us to approach the process of our *teshuvah* (turning, return, repentance, response, answer) as a quandary and as a question: *What* must we change and *what* must we perpetuate and repeat? How frightening it is to leave that which is familiar and comfortable and to jump into the abyss of the new and the unknown. Habit and routine, complacency and peace of mind, conventions and cliches constantly seduce us into pale, superficial lives, lacking in passion, substance and truth. How often we offer a resounding "No!" to risk, to venture, to struggle, to ambiguity, and settle for getting older without ever growing. And yet, can life be lived exclusively and permanently on the brink of challenge and change? It would be both simplistic and foolish to declare that everything needs to be uprooted and transformed. There is so much that deserves to be reiterated precisely because it is true and holy. Repetition is a prerequisite for learning and for approaching perfection. Repetition grants us familiarity, comfort, warmth, a soothing mainstay in the often terrifying face of living.

What must we repeat and *what* must we change? Repetition and change are each an abyss on either side of Rabbi Nahman of Bratzlav's *"gesher tzar me'od,"* the very narrow bridge of life. Yet, there is no alternative to the bridge if we choose to embrace life in all its reality and fullness. We pray on the High Holy Days that God allow us to journey on the bridge of life, give us the courage to ask the real questions, and the faith and discernment to respond. May we all be inscribed and sealed in the Book of Life. *Leshanah Tovah Tikatevu veTehatemu.*

– J. Rolando Matalon

High Holiday Preparation

Connecting Moment

Rabbi Roly Matalon

By the time the High Holy Days are over, you will have spent hours in synagogue and maybe you even had a few minutes or thirty seconds of something absolutely real and deep. But those hours are worth those few minutes or seconds. In those moments when we feel really connected, there is something transcendent that happens. I can't spell out the nature of that connection for you; it will be something unique and personal. It could be with God, with a deeper part of yourself, with the community, with the music, with the text, with your grandparents, with Israel, or with the language. There are limitless possibilities of how our connection can be sparked.

That moment of connection, however short or fleeting, is worth the hours invested searching for it. If it is a real connection, then there is nothing like it. You may get some insight into who you truly are or who you are meant to be. You might begin to discover who you are, not only psychologically and emotionally but also spiritually as a Jew. If you can make this connection, it is profound.

Our culture is a culture of immediate gratification; we want it and we want it now. And we want it for the least possible cost and with the least possible work. In the spiritual world it just doesn't happen like that. The deepest things require time and effort while taking the risk that nothing may happen this time. You went to *shul* one day and it did not happen. But it could happen next time so you have to show up again. If you insist on getting it immediately and when you don't you stop searching, you will never get it.

We resist the idea of putting in sustained effort to achieve connection. We want someone else to do the work for us. What we have to accept is that these things take preparation. They take reading, thinking, and preparing. They take coming to synagogue and putting in the time.

I think people have to know that and be willing to tolerate the uncertainty. We seek and we seek and we seek, but we never find. Maybe the problem is the way we are seeking. We are seeking too much in sync with the culture of which we are a part. We demand results too soon and too fast. The culture of instant gratification, of driving through, doesn't yield much.

To make a spiritual connection you have to give up the idea of immediate results. You have to be patient and commit to traveling down a road that can be long and widening and you need to suspend all critical judgment and all these expectations that it has to happen now. Suspend all that and just let yourself be in the experience.

Preparation

Rabbi Roly Matalon

You look at the enormity of the task: you have never opened up a prayer book and you don't know how to read Hebrew. You have never done it before, and since it is so intimidating you might abandon the whole thing even before you start. To keep from being overwhelmed, don't set the bar so high that you can't reach it. Start with doing a little bit, do some reading before. There are some wonderful resources available to help prepare for the High Holy Days. Different people have different internal landscapes and they are attracted to different perspectives. Go to a Jewish website or a Jewish bookstore, look around, and figure out what is compelling to you. Then choose something to read to prepare, even if it's just one or two things.

If you can't read Hebrew, look at a prayer book in translation. Some prayer books are annotated because the language of the prayers can be problematic. There are theological assumptions in the prayer book. There are gender issues; God is always in the masculine. It may sound too patriarchal. It may sound like the theology is outdated. But you don't have to read these things literally. There are some wonderful prayer books that are annotated to help people to transcend the limitations of language, gender, and theology.

If you can, take another step. Don't only read the prayer book, study it in a group. Many places offer lectures, sessions, or workshops before the holy days. Once you have done some learning, you have to go through the experience of going to synagogue. Try out different synagogues before the High Holy Days and see where you like the music, the community, and the style, etc. You should go in and out and explore options and pick the one where you feel most comfortable.

Once you have chosen a place, you have to show up on the High Holy Days. There are some logistical things to attend to. First of all, you have to call to see if they have room and whether you need a "ticket". You have to see how early you need to get there. These are mundane details, but they are important.

Once you have made the practical arrangements, go and attend for an hour. If an hour is too much then try for forty-five minutes. Push yourself beyond your level of comfort because, if you don't, you are not going to achieve anything. You are not going to let the experience take you where it needs to take you. If after half an hour you are tired and you quit, you are not going to get much. But if you push yourself beyond your comfort level, you may have a chance of achieving something. Sometimes after forty-five minutes, it might be painful, but wait another fifteen minutes, and maybe you will have broken a barrier and you can stay for another hour. Let the experience happen. Do not try to be in control and be critical and judgmental. Just let it go through you.

The Month Leading up to the High Holidays

Rabbi DovBer Pinson

Before we enter into an experience — any experience — we must prepare. This is especially true if we want the experience to have a deep and lasting impact and effect on us. For this to occur, we must attempt to enter into each experience with the appropriate mindset and be open to receive and integrate the fruits of that particular experience.

This insight is essential when considering how we should approach the High Holidays. If we want something real out of the experience, something deep and truly transformative, we need to put in the prior work necessary to prepare the soil of our soul for the seeds of the New Year.

For this very reason we have the month of Elul.

The entire month of Elul is set aside for serious soul-searching. It is a time, according to a psycho-spiritual reading of the Hebrew calendar, when we are asked to look deeply inward.

Elul is connected with the sign of Virgo, the virgin. This represents the idea of locating and reclaiming your inner innocence. In addition, the month of Elul is connected with the Hebrew letter *Yud*. *Yud* is the smallest Hebrew letter. In fact, it is taught that every single letter of the Hebrew alphabet begins with the letter *Yud*. *Yud* is the infinitesimal point and everything else is the manifestation, which follows from that point of origin.

What is the *Yud*? The *Yud* is the quality of wisdom and light that exists within every single form and manifestation of life. When you say that you are looking for the *Yud* in something, it means that you are looking for the innermost point of purity, wisdom, and purpose in that particular person, place, time, or thing.

The month of Elul is thus understood as an introduction to the month of Tishrei, and therefore, to the High Holidays. Before we enter into the High Holidays, before we appear before the Most High Merciful One, we must know, to the best of our ability, who we are.

Who are you? This is a serious question. We each want to know who we are, together and alone. In order to approach this kind of knowing, we must look deeply within ourselves and try to locate the *Yud* in each experience.

We may have had a hard year. We can look back at that year and at what happened and say, "Everything happened for a purpose." What was that purpose? What was that time or experience in life trying to teach you? Where was the *Yud* in all that? Where was the wisdom hidden in your past year? How can you learn from your past in order to grow? These are the kinds of questions we may ask during Elul in order to tap into that probing type of consciousness as we attempt to find that small *Yud*, waiting to be found within our life. This is how we prepare for Tishrei.

Before every sound there is a silence that precedes the sound. Elul is associated with "silence", which is the stillness that comes before the "sound" of Tishrei. This is illustrated by the fact that the Shofar is blown on Rosh Hashanah, the first day of the New Year directly following the final month of Elul. The Shofar blast is considered the 'first sound' of the year — the initiatory vibration that gives birth to the next cycle of creation. We learn from this that Elul is a time of transition, inward reflection and serious, spiritual work, which gives birth to the 'cry' of the birth of the New Year.

The silence that precedes the sound is the place of intuitive wisdom before a thought becomes articulated. In our own lives there is a lot of sound, a lot of noise, and a lot of commotion that happens. In the stillness of our inner-self we are able to sit and settle as we try to find the silence that precedes the sound. This is called soul-searching.

When we talk about soul-searching, which is represented by the month of Elul, we are not only talking about looking at the 'bad' or negative things we have done, or positive things you thought to do, but never got around to. Because if all your thoughts about yourself are negative, and all you think about is how bad you are, or that you are a failure who is incapable of change, then you will most likely continue reenacting those negative behavioral patterns.

So Elul is really about trying to find the blessings, wisdom, and goodness within your life and past year. If you believe that you are blessed and your life is a blessing, then you will be blessed and you will be a blessing. In Elul, we have to find that inner innocence, that point of purity, that baseline of blessing, and world of wisdom that we all have within our life, and through that we can empower ourselves to grown and to become even better people, partners, parents and protagonists in the coming year to follow.

12-Step Meditation for Elul

Rabbi DovBer Pinson

To properly prepare ourselves to enter into the New Year, or any new beginning for that matter, we need to consciously deal with all that is old, stale, and outdated in our lives before we can fully move into the future. We do this by engaging in a process referred to by the sages as *Chesbon Ha'Nefesh* or "Accounting of the Soul".

Cheshbon Ha'Nefesh occurs when we survey the past year, own up to each experience, and take responsibility for all that has transpired. It is only then, after we have gathered up and grabbed a hold of our past year in all its details that we can really let it all go so that we can move forward into the promise of a new future.

It is commonly understood that we cannot progress if we are stuck to our past, a full cup cannot be filled. To truly begin anew, the old reality must be put to rest.

So as Rosh Hashanah is approaching, we should do a complete review of the past year, and when Rosh Hashanah begins we can let it go and move on. A true Cheshbon Ha'Nefesh requires us to go through the year, month by month, to review, reclaim, and refine all of our past experiences. As we do this, there are a few helpful hints that we can keep in mind to organize and contextualize the details of this spiritual accounting.

Each month of the year has a particular energy, so while you go through the past year month by month, you can think about a particular month, as well as all the issues of the year that are related to the energy of that month. This means that if it's a time of thinking about relationships for example, corresponding to the month of Teves, you can think about the relationships of that particular month, but also about all the relationships you had over the past year. Awareness of each month's energy/quality can serve to focus your reflection upon a particular month, as well as provide an archetypal perspective upon the many dimensions of a full year.

This is especially important for the final 12 days of the month of Elul, as each day corresponds to a particular month of the year. Elul comes at the end of the solar cycle, as counted by the Hebrew calendar, and before the new Solar year begins. So at the end of that cycle, for the final 12 days, we reflect upon and revisit the past year. This is similar to the first month of the lunar cycle, as counted by the Hebrew calendar, the month of Nisan, wherein the first 12 days of the month correspond to the 12 upcoming months of the year. So at the beginning of the next cycle, for the first 12 days, we project and envision positivity and blessing for the upcoming year. We can see from these two transitional moments that every changing season (physically and spiritually), is a time to take account, to either look back upon the past, or to project into the future.

Included below is a list of the Hebrew months, their corresponding qualities, and some suggested questions for reflection.

To begin, gently close your eyes and review your past year, month by month, starting with last year's Tishrei and moving on from there:

1) **Tishrei** (Sep-Oct): *Resolutions and Commitments* — What resolutions did you take upon yourself last year? What promises did you make last Tishrei? What goals did you set? Have you achieved them?

2) **Chesvan** (Oct-Nov): *Transformation* — During this time the seasons change and turn from fall to winter, it gets colder and darker. Think about the transformations in your life that occurred last year? Which were your own doing and which were situational or circumstantial? How did you respond to the challenges of change?

3) **Kislev** (Nov-Dec): *Miracles* — Think about the miracles in your life. What extraordinary events happened to you last year? Did you find a spouse, fall in love, land a dream job, or

make a significant breakthrough? How did you handle these miracles and movements? Did you integrate them? Were you thankful for them as they occurred?

4) **Teves** (Dec-Jan): *Relationships* — How were your relationships this past year? Think about your parents, siblings, spouse, children, friends, co-workers, even 'enemies.' Did you improve your interpersonal relationships with others? Where did you fall short? Where were your successes?

5) **Shevat** (Jan-Feb): *Eating* — Eating is one of the primary appetites that we must work on to refine our character and live a truly conscious and spiritual life. How was your relationship to food this past year? Healthy? Obsessive? Disciplined? Neurotic? Were you able to let go and enjoy yourself when appropriate? Were you able to exert your will and define your boundaries when necessary?

6) **Adar** (Feb-Mar): *Joy* — What were the truly joyous moments of your past year? What made you laugh? What made you sing? What made you dance? What made you weep with joy? Did you grow or learn from the joy you experienced in the past year?

7) **Nisan** (Mar-Apr): *Redemption and Liberation* — Think about the issues in your life that you were able to release yourself from this past year. This can be in the form of certain difficulties that you overcame, particular patterns or habits that you broke, or relationships you evolved from or evolved within. Do you feel truly free from them? If not,

what else might you still need to do to more fully move on?

8) **Iyyar** (Apr-May): *Healing* — Healing is being true to yourself on the deepest level. What ailments or challenges did you experience over the past year? What did you do to help or hurt your own healing process? Remember that healing can happen on all levels of your being. Don't just confine this reflection to the physical realm. Go deep.

9) **Sivan** (May-Jun): *Torah* — What have you learned this year? Have you integrated those teachings? Did you truly "receive" the Torah this past year?

10) **Tamuz** (Jun-July): *Destruction* — It was during this month that the 'walls of the Temple' were breached. Although the Temple does not fully fall until the month of Av, we meditate on the process and beginnings of disintegration during the month of Tamuz. Think about all the losses you experienced in your past year. What have you lost? Whom have you lost? How are you dealing with these losses?

11) **Av** (July-Aug): *Reconciliation* — Although most commonly characterized by the total destruction of both the first and second Temples, we choose to focus on the perennial question, "what next?" that follows complete collapse. This corresponds to the teaching that "the Moshiach is born on Tisha B'Av", the day of complete destruction. What restorative steps did you pursue last year in broken areas of your life? How have you tried to repair or redeem aspects of yourself, your relationships, or the world? Have you volunteered your time or energy to people in need? Have you

reached out to someone you have not been in contact with for a long time? How are these projects or processes going?

12) **Elul** (Aug-Sept): *Soul Searching* — Have you been honest with yourself this past year? Were you able to really look at your life and yourself deeply and critically? Were you able to judge yourself favorably and lovingly? Think about the times that you were really honest with yourself, how did it feel?

Once you have gone through the year, owning up to and taking responsibility for all your mishaps and successes, now it is time to move into the more proactive consciousness of looking at the present as a gift of the eternal now — literally a new beginning.

When we begin anew, and we can always 'begin' again at any moment, we need to think that, in the words of Rabbeinu Yonah, "*The foundation of teshuvah is considering today as the very day you were born, the first day of your life, and you have no demerits or merits.*"

Every moment is new. The *Ko'ach ha-Hischadshus,* or 'Power of Renewal', is present within every moment of Creation. There are no two moments alike. Yet, at the same time, all the newness of the entire year flows from Rosh Hashanah. Rosh Hashanah is the reservoir and wellspring of newness and initiation that ripples out to the rest of the year. Now is the time to activate and access that initiatory energy.

This means that Rosh Hashanah brings down newness for the entire year. *Rosh Hashanah*, which literally means 'Head of the Year', is not just a beginning or a starting line, but a head. And just as the head contains the consciousness of all that transpires in the body, so too *Rosh Hashanah* is that essential node through which all the vitality of an entire year travels.

Rosh Hashanah is the renewal of time, as well as the nerve center through which all directions of time flow. On *Rosh Hashanah*, there is a total cosmic renewal, and by attuning ourselves to this awesome day, we can achieve a sense of renewed vitality on all levels of our being — a radical renewal in time, space, and soul (consciousness).

The Spiritual Nature of the Month of Tishrei

Rabbi DovBer Pinson

There is something very interesting about the Hebrew name of the month of *Tishrei*. The first letters that spell out the name Tishrei (*taf, shin, reish*) are the final three letters of the Hebrew *alpeh-bet*, but in reverse order. According to the Kabbalah, letters are transmitters of energy, of information, and of divine life force.

Normally the structure of energy would start with an *aleph* (first letter), and flow out into a *beis* (second letter), and continue all the way down the *aleph-bet* finally arriving at *taf*. There is actually a narrative structure that runs through the Hebrew *aleph-bet*, which tells the tale of creation. Seen in this light, *aleph* would be Infinity reaching out to touch the Finite, the first 'expression' in form, and *taf* would be the final manifestation in form. So the whole letter formation from *aleph* to *taf* indicates a flow of energy in a downward trajectory or direction.

When things are spelled in reverse, with the last letter first, it represents that there is a movement from down—up. This is understood as 'reversing the flow'. You are starting at the bottom, with *taf*, and moving your way back up the ladder. The Kabbalists refer to this as an "arousal from below". The entire month of Tishrei is about remembering how to self-generate, and about how we, the 'final manifestation of form', can move back towards the *aleph*, towards the Creator, towards the Infinite.

If you look closely at the High Holidays in Tishrei, you will see that nothing 'miraculous' happened here. This is opposed to Passover, Purim, Chanukah, or even Shavuot when we received the Torah. During the High Holidays, we are celebrating our very creation, as well as our opportunity to be co-creative. During this season we are reclaiming our ability to transform, which is powerful indeed, but not by itself miraculous. We are not celebrating the splitting of the sea for example, or the saving of our people from annihilation. We are celebrating our inherent connection to the Source.

We are stating unequivocally that our stories, our communities, our struggles, have value; our life has worth. It is our birthday, and today we take responsibility for all that is human.

We are celebrating that we, the finite, can rise and move upward towards the highest Heights. Instead of the energy flowing from the top down, we are actually reversing the flow and redirecting the cosmic flow of consciousness upward, back to its Source in the Infinite One.

Think of a student learning from a teacher. In the presence of the teacher, the student completely understands what the teacher has said. But when the student leaves the room and someone asks him, "What did your teacher say?" He has forgotten everything. But in the presence of the teacher, he remembers everything.

Nisan is the month in which we are given a gift, the Divine Presence, which miraculously lifts us up and out of our constrictions and entrapments. During this time, we were liberated from Egypt, both literally and figuratively. The metaphorical Egypt refers to all of our inner constrictions and limitations. In this process the sea split, both literally and inwardly, and our inner visions became revealed on the external level. And yet, because of this miraculous dynamic, Nisan is not a time where we learn how to 'get free', because we are just given it as a gift. Tishrei is the time when we move upward gradually, from the bottom—up. Tishrei is the time when we decide that we want the connection, and we do whatever it takes to make it. Nissan teaches us how to depend on the Above, and Tishrei teaches us how to motivate and depend on ourselves for our spiritual growth and refinement. But both months carry one similar message: Never give up!

Tishrei is characterized by the idea of generating something from within ourselves. In this way, we are participating in the process of self-refinement, and not just passively receiving the product of that process. That is why the month of Tishrei is symbolized by the image of the Scales of Judgment (Libra), which is the idea of balance. The true balance of life is achieved when we are able to take inspiration from Above or from outside of ourselves, and then to couple that inspiration with perspiration, which is the drive that comes from within and manifests as our active participation in making a tangible difference in our own lives and within the world. It is not enough to take something that was given to us and put it on a shelf somewhere to be forgotten or neglected. We must exert ourselves on all levels as we work and participate in our own process of growth and evolution.

Rosh Hashanah is, essentially, this idea of judgment. On the deepest level, it is the ability to self-reflect and self-judge your life and actions — to ask yourself who you are and what is your purpose.

Yom Kippur is then best understood as the time when you come to encounter yourself as you really are without any add-ons, attachments, or addendums. To do this we strip away all of our externals. We don't eat, we put on white garments, we do not have intimacy, we don't work. We must strip away all the false images and definitions of self, in order to really ask, "who am I right now?

If I take away all the things that surround me and that I surround myself with food, clothes, job, relationships, etc., who am I as a person? What is my identity?" Yom Kippur is the time to really encounter your self.

During the time of the High Holidays, we need to really be asking ourselves, "Who am I? What is my purpose? How can I connect with something much Larger and Loftier than me?"

High Holidays 101

David Solomon

It is impossible to convey in words the essential meaning of Rosh Hashanah and Yom Kippur because their essential meaning is ultimately experiential. What is unique about that period is that it gives us the opportunity to stand as human beings before the Creator of the universe. On Rosh Hashanah, we do not stand before God the redeemer; we stand before God the Creator, as Abraham stood before God when he realized that it is possible to have a relationship with the Creator of the universe. It is true that "*Hashem huh HaElokim*," the God who redeems within history is the God who is the Creator of the universe. But on Rosh Hashanah our main task is to be renewed with the recreation of the world; to justify its recreation. The key that links creation and redemption is the concept of *teshuva*, one of the most unique, spiritual concepts that the Jewish people have given the world. *Teshuva* is a dynamic movement that begins with an inner transformation/recreation and from the individual, transforms/recreates society and ultimately the universe itself.

Elevated Prayer

Rabbi Roly Matalon

People go to synagogue for their different reasons. There are social reasons. Sometimes people go to find community. It is important that the synagogue is a place where you find other seekers and you connect with them socially. Marking Shabbat, holidays, and life cycle events, whether happy or sad, require community. You cannot live Judaism alone. There are family reasons. Your parents, grandparents, in-laws will be there, and there can be social expectations.

But deeper than that, there is a place in our hearts that longs for a deep connection and aspires to change. This is not restricted to Jews, Muslims, Christians or Buddhists. Every human being, when they allow themselves, wants to aspire, to change, to grow, to hope. You want more out of your life. You want something more intense, deeper, beautiful, and holy. That is the beginning of true prayer. You peel off the social and family reasons and you come to that core: the human being who aspires. We all have some brokenness in our heart. We all have things we are not happy with. There are things in our lives that pain us. So we reach into that place that is broken and that place that aspires. That is where things begin to happen with prayer.

I believe the way the prayer book was conceived by our sages enables us to reach those places. But it takes time to reach that place. That is why services are long. The experience of prayer is like peeling an onion. You peel layer after layer, till you get to a center. But you cannot get there immediately it does not work by cutting it in the middle. It only works by peeling. So the first part of the service, you are in some place in those concentric circles. You break through the layers as the service goes on. The prayer book is designed to help us do that work and to get to that core, that center, that concealed place of brokenness, aspiration, hope, and longing.

Prayer is about reaching that place. What is said exactly is not that important. We have a prayer book which has worked for many generations. Maybe we need to tweak it here and there. The language or the gender of God might be a problem to some. The fact that the matriarchs are absent is a barrier for many people. So we may need to tweak that technology but in general, it works. It is accompanied by music, reading of the Torah, and by teachings. All should be for the sake of helping us reach our core. When we can stand on that site of brokenness in our own hearts while simultaneously longing for repair and healing, we feel the connection we seek. Have confidence that you can find the faith and commitment to reach that place. There is a presence that is there with you, that we call God. God wants you to repair it. God is with you because God wants you to bridge the gaps and fulfill those longings. Then you want to continue, to keep going toward deeper and deeper places. That is the spiritual journey.

Prayer is meant to help us reach that place in our core.

Maybe this time you can reach it for a split second and then you want to try to reach it again. It might take you a few hours till you are there the next time. It takes a lot of work. That is why it cannot be done if you treat services like a drive through. Maybe some people can, I can't. I have never seen anyone that can do it. Maybe some spiritual giants can do it that quickly but probably not. Spiritual giants are able to stay with the hard journey until they reach that place.

Elevated Prayer

Rabbi DovBer Pinson

In Hebrew, the word for prayer is *tefilah* — suggesting that prayer is an act of *tofel*, of 'connecting and joining'. When we pray we are reaching out, beyond ourselves, beyond the immediate, and attempting to connect with the Infinite One Source of All Life. We pray because we feel the existential, inner urge to connect, to reach out, to communicate, to unify.

In English, the word "prayer" is employed to describe various religious and/or spiritual activities such as petition, penitence, praise, protest, thanksgiving, confession, contemplation, introspection and evaluation. Indeed, the act of prayer itself is likened to a blossoming tree with voluminous branches and plentiful fruit. This poetic image suggests that prayer is a multi-dimensional process that is fertile, gradual and rewarding. It is both an experience and an expression that resonates and reverberates in many worlds at once.

The above are just some of the potential pathways of prayer, but still the question remains: "What is the essence of prayer?"

For starters, we need to remember that when we pray, not only do we acknowledge that there is an Other to whom we can direct our prayers, but, more importantly, that this Other is actually aware of us, cares about us, and is worthy of our love and constant consideration.

Furthermore, along the lines of connecting self to soul or earth to heaven, prayer is likened to the ladder in Jacob's dream: a structure set upon the earth, with the top of it reaching to heaven. As we move ever upward, we simultaneously move deeper inward.

Appropriately, prayer is referred to in the Gemarah as *avodah she'ba'lev* — 'a service of the heart'. In fact, prayer is an active expression of the heart that happens through the heart, as well as within the heart. When we genuinely pray, there is a movement both inward and upward — connecting us to our deepest, most vulnerable self, and in turn, connecting that Self with the Most High Ultimate Source of All Reality.

Prayer is a selfless service that can potentially penetrate deep into the depths of our broken hearts if we are only able to open ourselves up and pray with total emotional involvement and honesty.

There are times when the desire to pray is aroused spontaneously and feels like one of the most natural forms of human expression. And yet, at other times, it is difficult to pray and challenging to truly open up. The art of authentic prayer requires that we are completely present and focused on the ultimate undertaking. Having *Kavanah*, 'Intention', is essential to prayer. Intention is the soul of prayer. Prayer without intention is likened to "a body without a soul."

Yet, a distinction should be made between the essence of prayer and the technique of prayer. The technique of prayer is there to point us in the right direction so that we can truly reach out, connect, and unify with the Source of all Life. Intentions and instructions set the coordinates, but there needs to be someone steering the ship, someone who is actively praying the prayer, and someone who is giving the words *ruach*, or 'spirit'. That someone is you.

Prayer offers us the opportunity to unabashedly express our feelings, needs, fears, and desires in front of our Creator. Not merely as a hollow and meaningless monologue, but as a conscious and meaningful gesture upon entering into genuine dialogue. Prayer is the time we take and the space we make to "hear" the Creator "speaking" to and through us.

While standing in the midst of deep prayer, we should be filled with an overwhelming awareness that we are in the presence of the Infinite One. In turn, we may find that the ego-walls of self-delusion and deception come tumbling down. Who we are and what we truly desire become increasingly clear when the garments and games of our ego are eliminated.

From one perspective, prayer is intended to petition the Creator for things that we cannot acquire on our own. But when seen from a deeper perspective, we find that, through the very act of asking, we become more aware of what we really do want and need. We gain access to a more reflective awareness of ourselves, and our desires, through the very act of prayer.

When we pray with genuine vulnerability and open communication, we can no longer fool ourselves. When we courageously reveal ourselves to God, our life becomes increasingly more transparent. It is only when we have reached this place of clarity, honesty, and humility that the deep inner work of self-improvement can truly begin.

The High Holidays

High Holidays

Rabbi Roly Matalon

The High Holidays come at the very beginning of the year. They are part of a "spiritual technology" that allows us to do two things. First, look into the year that we are ending and do some sort of spiritual stock-taking, an evaluation. We see where we have succeeded, where we have failed, what we should keep, and what we should change. We should evaluate this on different levels: our relationship with God, our family, our community, the world, the people of Israel, and the environment. In all those circles of relationships we look at where we have been, what we have done, what have we contributed, what have we learned, how have we grown, where we have ascended, and where we have descended. Through prayer, reflection, *teshuva*, and everything we surround ourselves with during the holy days, we forge a vision for the year to come. It is not only where have I been but where I want to be. Where do I want to grow? Which places need more of my attention within myself and also in my relationships? To what should I devote myself? Where should I put more attention? What vulnerabilities do I need to attend to? This is how we do the second part of the work of the High Holy days, forging an intention and vision for the year to come.

Tradition calls the High Holy Days the Days of Judgment. During these days, we use the spiritual technology of the prayerbook to examine our lives. But our introspection doesn't take place in isolation or in some sort of bubble. We do it within a community. The prayerbook also invites us to look outside of ourselves. It maps an internal journey while providing us with huge windows looking outside into the spiritual and material world. It helps us see ourselves and connects us to something much greater. That is what the prayer book is about during the High Holy Days.

There are so many levels to this journey. The thing is that if you really take this journey, it is a difficult one. It is exacting, demanding, and painful because you see things about yourself that are not always pleasant. You see yourself truly, with all your successes but also with all your weaknesses and failures. That is not easy it is hard and lonely.

That is another reason to undertake this spiritual work within a community. When we are in the company of people who are also taking this journey and our journeys intersect, our lives intersect. I know that you are doing the same work so I take courage from the fact that we are all doing this work together, and together we are looking at a vision for a better, more meaningful, and deeper life. We are all envisioning a better world. If you could for a minute take God's perspective, and see all of these people doing this spiritual work at the same time, all across the world, it would be amazing. All people want to grow and change. They all want to have more meaningful lives; they are all trying to go to deeper places, bring good in the world, and refuse to settle for the ways things are.. They want to bring in *tikkun* (rectification). It is awe-inspring.

This is a holy time, it is a time pregnant with opportunity and possibility. That is what the beginning of the year is about. It is not just about popping some bottles and getting drunk like on the secular New Year. There is something appealing about that kind of complete abandon which is filled with celebration and gratitude. But the High Holy Days are much more than that.

When we forge our vision and intention for the year ahead, we know it is going to be a hard road. So we need to fill ourselves with courage. Being in a community, praying and singing together, is powerful. The words of the prayers are so holy and deep. They have been sanctified by generations who have given themselves to these words. We bring these words, we recite and say them, and from that, we can derive the faith and the courage we need. We need faith to be able to then walk on the path we have envisioned. Most of us set high goals- we set the bar high because we really want to jump over it and improve. It hurts to live down low. We have a lot to be grateful for, but at the same time we all have pain in our lives. We want to overcome it. We want to move ahead in big leaps. It takes a lot of strength. The holidays can give us that strength. When Yom Kippur concludes, anyone that has done the work feels it, it energizes you. You are tired from fasting and an entire day of prayer. Even if you only pray a little but you do it with intensity, you are tired. But at the same time you are revitalized, recharged and you are ready to move forward.

Days of Awe

Rabbi DovBer Pinson

The High Holidays are called *Yamim Noraim*, which literally translates as "Days of Awe." But to fully understand what this oft-repeated phrase refers to, we have to unpack what "awe" means. What does it mean to stand in awe?

Forty days before Yom Kippur is the first day of Elul. Thus begins the Days of Awe. We can see from this counting that the *Yamim Noraim* incorporate both the process of deep inner work and soul searching that commences with Elul, as well as the culminating state of pure presence and transparency that we strive for on Yom Kippur. Forty is a powerful number that reminds us of both revelation and repentance. Moshe was up on the mountain for forty days to receive the first set of tablets, as well as the second set. During the forty days of the *Yamim Noraim*, we strive to receive the revelation that results from true repentance.

But what does all this have to do with "Awe?" Awe is that moment when you stop being defined by or contained within only your 'self', and thus enter into a state of being that is much larger and more expansive. Let's say, for instance, that I'm in awe of a painting or a sunset. The actual moment in which I am in awe of that painting, before I attempt to conceptualize or understand why I'm in awe, I am completely lost in the experience of the painting. The idea of the *Yamim Noraim* is to get lost in a process and reality that is much more comprehensive than any one of us alone. For truly, it is through the experience of losing your self that you are able to then find yourself.

But before you go and lose your self in the midst of something so much more immense than little old you, you want to make sure that you are present. It is then that we ask the primary questions, "Who am I? Where am I?"

The entire month of *Elul* is dedicated to serious soul-searching. Elul is about finding out who you really are as a human being and as a Jew? You do not want to lose your self before you know who you are. First you have to know who you are and then you can stand in awe during those awesome days.

We can learn from this that there is both a gradual process of sensitizing ourselves to the experience of a state of awe, as well as the experience itself. To return to the metaphor of the painting, or any artistic experience for that matter, imagine meditating for an hour, or reflecting before visiting a museum in order to prepare yourself to be 'blown away'. This is the kind of mind-state that the full forty Days of Awe seeks to instill in us. That we should take the experience seriously, as well as taking our role in that experience seriously. It is a common saying, but one that rings true, that 'you get out of it what you put into it.' This is an important dynamic to keep in mind when contemplating the *Yamim Noraim*.

There are a handful practices that were done throughout Jewish history to do just this — to prepare for the potential 'lift-off' of Rosh Hashanah and Yom Kippur.

One example is the daily blowing of the *Shofar* throughout the month of Elul leading up to Rosh Hashanah. It is a very simple exercise. You just take a ram's horn and you give it a blow — that is the sound of the *Shofar*. The idea of the sound of the *Shofar* is to create focus. Sometimes people are talking in a room and someone gives a scream or you hear a siren, and everyone all of a sudden pays attention. Everyone's awareness is then focused on that person or siren.

The sound of the *Shofar* is that one sound that creates focused energy. This is true when it is blown in a group setting, as well as when it is blown privately. "I am scattered all over the place, I have a lot of noise in my life, I do this, I do that. I want to have one moment where I say wow!"

That one moment that you say 'wow' in the midst of a visceral cry, you are completely present in that crying. A moment later you may start asking yourself and analyzing, "Why am I crying? What hurt me?" But the first moment you are in pain, you are completely present in that pain. Elul is that time when we want to get into that experience of total absorption, to get into that moment when you are fully present with yourself. In this state you might say to yourself, "I am right here. I'm totally present. I am not over there or somewhere else. Right now, I am in the exact place that I need to be. Where am I, right now, right here?"

That is the idea of the sound of the *Shofar*. The sound evokes the awareness that I am completely present in that 'wow' moment. Soul search and look deeply into yourself: What do I have to continue to work on and perfect? Feel being fully present in that vulnerable state. Blow the Shofar. Let the sound and vibration focus your attention and intention. The consciousness that immediately follows the sound is the silent shout of the 'wow!' That is the sound of *Shofar*.

In order to be present throughout the gradual process of soul-searching, so that you can be present at the transformative time of the high holidays, it would also be a good idea to try another practice known as, *Tannis Dibur*, or "Fasting from Speech".

Speech is a beautiful tool that has tremendous value. But sometimes we can get lost in all the sound and static. We are often able to avoid issues by just talking, this is otherwise known as idle chatter. Someone asks you how you are doing and you start rambling on about various topics, but you are not answering the real questions — "How are you? Where are you?" Speech, when utilized as a form of distraction, is a great way to ignore serious issues in your life.

But when you fill your life with ceaseless chatter, and then you walk into a quiet room or you are alone driving in your car and it is completely quiet, you become uncomfortable. In such a situation you have nowhere to turn, you have to encounter yourself and you do not want to. Right away you need a distraction and you put on some music.

The time of Elul is an opportunity to practice moments of meaningful silence. They can last for ten minutes, an hour, two hours, or as long as you want. Become comfortable in your own presence in silence without having to express yourself or feel the need to fill that space with sound.

Create silence in your life. Before you go to sleep is an excellent time to say the blessing over sleep, or to say the *Shema*, and then attempt to be quiet for the rest of the night. You will most likely be uncomfortable at first, because you may not know how to be in the silence. Most people get their sense of identity from the noise around them, from all the stimuli that surrounds them. The idea of Elul is to disregard all the noise and the external stimuli and to try to find out who you are as a human being, as a Jew, as a soul. Who are you all alone in those moments of silence?

We can see from these two practices that there are two opposite things going on during the month of Elul. On one hand we are creating noise, a very loud and primal noise in fact, which is the sound of the *Shofar*. It is neither verbal nor conceptual. It is the focused sound of a guttural cry and visceral wailing that will focus your energy. The context from which such a sound comes from is silence. By achieving a state of peace and quiet and stillness within ourselves we become focused on that one place, that inner point, the *Yud*.

If we can enter into the High Holidays properly prepared then we increase the chances of having a truly deep and transformative experience. Otherwise Rosh Hashanah is basically just going through the motions — going to the synagogue, talking to your friends, having a nice dinner, and it means nothing more than an insincere nod to your friend.

In order for Rosh Hashanah to be transformational, you need to feel like you have been judged thoroughly and inwardly. In truth, you have judged yourself. If you want to really feel forgiven during Yom Kippur, you have to go and involve yourself in the experience. It is not simply a gift. It is not something that is given to us. It is something we have to strive for.

When we enter that potentially transcendent place on Rosh Hashanah we have to be prepared for such an experience. As a result of our preparations, we are much more likely to be able to access and integrate the awesome experience in a more substantial way. For truly, even Rosh Hashanah and Yom Kippur are preparations to truly experience the joy and ecstasy of *Simchas Torah*, which is the final celebration of the Tishrei holidays. In order to be able to receive the Torah and understand that happiness, we need to have built ourselves and have become the proper vessels. This is the true celebration of pure holy joy.

If we can go through the whole cycle of experiences in the encounter of self, stripping ourselves of all our negativity and standing fearless and naked, then we can fully be embraced by the four walls of the *Sukkah* which represent the four letters of Hashem's name. Once we feel fully unified within the Divine Presence, we can end the holidays on a very joyous note, and begin the next cycle in a blessed and balanced way.

It poses the question in a Chassidic text, "how do you know if Yom Kippur was successful? How do you know if after an entire day of fasting and praying you were forgiven?" If the moment that Yom Kippur is over you feel a tremendous amount of inner joy, then it was successful. If you feel more connected to the anticipated food and during the break-fast you are pushing, shoving, and aggressively reaching over people to get something to eat, you might as well go back and start Yom Kippur all over again.

If you can experience true joy after Yom Kippur then you know it was successful. If by the end of Tishrei you can truly experience *Simchas Torah*, the "Joy of the Torah", in an eternal and joyful way, then the process was fruitful and you may taste from the *Eitz Chaim*, "The Tree of Life". The ultimate lesson of the *Yamim Noraim* is that deep spiritual work and growth is not something that is given to you, but must be self-generated. If you can feel that and rise to its challenge, then you have gone through the holidays in a meaningful and transformative way.

Rosh Hashanah & Yom Kippur

Rabbi Joseph Telushkin

1) Rabbis Byron Sherwin and Seymour Cohen write: "One of the most popular and regularly observed rituals in America is the annual medical checkup. Each year, millions of people are examined, tested, and evaluated in order to determine the state of their physical health and well being. Often, one fasts in preparation for a variety of tests and procedures.... If an illness is detected or if a potential illness is indicated, a modification of one's behavior is required. When sickness is diagnosed, a regimen is prescribed to help restore health. What may be ascertained during the examination period can lead to a change of life-style for the rest of the year, indeed, for the remainder of one's life. During the High Holiday season, Jews undergo a kind of 'spiritual checkup.' Prayer, fasting, and introspection are meant to be catalysts to aid one in evaluating the state of one's spiritual [and moral] health. This process is called *teshuva*, repentance."[1]

2) Because the following exercise is painful, many people may try to avoid doing it. Yet this procedure, more than almost any other, can help us prepare for the High Holidays.

Start with the sentence, "What I regret having done in the last year is..." and list the things you wish you had done differently or not done at all. The list can include such items as:

> I didn't visit my friend who was sick with cancer;
>
> I let a friendship drop because it would not help me socially or professionally, and might even hold me back;
>
> I misled someone in a financial transaction;
>
> I didn't return a phone call, or several calls, to someone who really needed to talk to me;
>
> I didn't make an effort to help someone get a job, even though I had a connection that might have helped them.

Rabbi Abraham Twerski – from whom I first learned of this idea – suggests that writing out this personal confession can be more effective and personally meaningful than simply reciting the general confession shared by all in the prayerbook (*al chet*, "for the sin I committed by...").[2]

3) Another difficult act, but one that will help cleanse our soul: We should make peace with someone with whom we have had a falling-out, particularly if the person is a family member.

In many families, there are people – first cousins or even brothers and sisters – who are not on speaking terms. I urge people to take advantage of the High Holiday period of forgiveness to make at least an initial, even if seemingly superficial, peace with the other party (during the course of the year the peace may well grow deeper). For one thing, unless your sibling or other close relative is a hard-core criminal or a highly abusive person, it is a great act of disrespect to your parents, whether they are living or dead, to disassociate from close family members. As a parent, I know how important it is to me that my children love and care for each other. Among the greatest tragedies I could imagine would be to learn that my children were no longer on speaking terms. Therefore, the fulfillment of the Fifth Commandment, to "Honor your father and mother," mandates that, except in the most extreme instances, we do not break off contact with a close family member.

Also, there is something hypocritical about coming to synagogue on the High Holidays and beseeching God to look upon us favorably and treat us with mercy and forgiveness, if we are unwilling to act that way to others. The Talmud teaches that God forgives the sins of those who don't hold grudges and who forgive offenses committed against them (*Rosh Hashana* 17a). Only if we act in a forgiving manner toward others do we make ourselves worthy of God's forgiveness.

This Jewish tradition, of a holiday devoted to seeking forgiveness and granting it, is one I believe we should try and influence our non-Jewish neighbors to adopt. Perhaps the United States could establish a National Apology Day, during which people would seek out those they had hurt, and ask for forgiveness. Such a day might be scheduled for December, so that people could end one year and start a new one with something approaching a clean slate. By having an annual date when an offender has reason to believe that many others will seek forgiveness and that the hurt parties will be more open to granting it, the embarrassed offender might more easily be ready to approach the person whom she has hurt.

4) Perhaps the most famous sentence in the High Holiday liturgy underscores the three acts that Jewish tradition teaches are most likely to secure God's forgiveness: *Teshuvah, tefilah, tzedakah,* "Repentance, prayer, and charity can avert the severity of the evil decree" (from the *Machzor,* the High Holiday prayerbook). Engage in all three acts during the ten days between Rosh Hashanah and Yom Kippur.

5) Yet another High Holiday prayer reminds us that "all of your deeds are written down in a book" (*ve-kol ma'asecha ba-sefer nichtavim*). As the Talmud teaches: "When a person comes to his eternal world, all of his earthly actions are enumerated before him" (*Ta'anit* 11a).

6) Jewish tradition encourages us to act with particular piety, kindness, and generosity during the *Aseret Y'mei Teshuva* (the Ten Days of Repentance), the period of time starting with Rosh Hashana, and concluding with Yom Kippur. Many Jews presume that God will reward them in the year ahead if they act righteously during this ten-day period. Does such a belief make sense, the notion that if we behave well during these ten days, but do not continue to do so after Yom Kippur, we will fool God into believing that we are worthy of divine kindness?

Rabbi David Woznica speculates that the demands made of

Jews during the *Aseret Y'mei Teshuva* have less to do with impressing God than with teaching people how good they can be. Thus, if you were to ask people to make permanent changes in their lives:

> Never again speak a word of *lashon hara*;
>
> Never again ignore a beggar;
>
> Always be patient with your family and with those around you;
>
> Whenever you pray, keep your mind fully focused on the prayer's meaning;

Most people, realizing that they could not follow such advice forever, would give up in advance, and not even make the effort. But if we ask people – including ourselves – to act this way for just ten days, many will make an effort. In the process, we will not only do much good, but we will also learn that we can be much better people than we thought possible. And such a realization can bring about an improvement in our behavior that will last well beyond the ten days.

So, this year, during the *Aseret Y'mei Teshuva* make a particular effort to give more money to charity than you normally do, refrain from losing your temper with your family and co-workers, focus with real concentration on your prayers, and try to go for these two-hundred-and-forty-hours without saying an unkind word about or to anyone.

A final thought

7) One of the best-known prayers recited on Yom Kippur is the confessional prayer known as the *Al Chet*, "For the sin I committed by..." On this day, Jews confess repeatedly to forty-four different transgressions. The awareness of how many sins we routinely commit, can, however, overwhelm some of us with a sense of guilt and despair. I suggest, therefore, that we also focus on the good things we do, and the good things we can do. Hence, the following – entitled, "For the Mitzvah We Performed" – is a suggested reading for the Yom Kippur service, that can be read aloud by a congregation or recited and studied individually:

1. For the *mitzvah* we performed by remembering the good someone did for us even when we were upset with him or her;

2. For the *mitzvah* we performed by stopping our child from teasing, humiliating, or calling another child by a hurtful nickname;

3. For the *mitzvah* we performed by standing up for justice when we saw someone mistreated;

4. For the *mitzvah* we performed by refusing to buy anything produced by child labor;

5. For the *mitzvah* we performed by remembering to express gratitude to anyone who helped us;

6. For the *mitzvah* we performed when we heard an

ambulance siren and offered a prayer to God on behalf of the sick person inside;

7. For the *mitzvah* we performed by knowing embarrassing information about someone and not passing it on;

8. For the *mitzvah* we performed when we gave food or money to someone who said he was hungry;

9. For the *mitzvah* we performed by donating charity cheerfully

10. For the *mitzvah* we performed by apologizing to one of our children whose feelings we had unfairly hurt;

All these things God, please remember and inspire us to do more acts like these in the year ahead.

11. For the *mitzvah* we performed by blessing our children on Shabbat and on the Jewish holidays;

12. For the *mitzvah* we performed by returning a lost object to its owner;

13. For the *mitzvah* we performed by visiting a sick person and offering emotional support to him and his family;

14. For the *mitzvah* we performed by helping someone to find work;

15. For the *mitzvah* we performed by teaching our children Torah;

16. For the *mitzvah* we performed by studying Torah ourselves;

17. For the *mitzvah* we performed by reserving our highest praise of our children for when they do kind deeds;

18. For the *mitzvah* we performed by hearing a negative rumor about someone and not passing it on;

19. For the *mitzvah* we performed by not encouraging our children to make friends with, or date, wealthy people, just because they are rich;

20. For the *mitzvah* we performed by refraining from snapping at the person who has chosen to share our life – our spouse;

All these things God, please remember and inspire us to do more acts like these in the year ahead.

21. For the *mitzvah* we performed by forgiving those who hurt us and sought our forgiveness;

22. For the *mitzvah* we performed by helping a developmentally disabled person find work;

23. For the *mitzvah* we performed by not exaggerating the bad traits of those with whom we disagree or whom we dislike;

24. For the *mitzvah* we performed by striving to be punctual even when it was difficult, so as to avoid keeping someone waiting;

25. For the *mitzvah* we performed by interacting with non-Jews in a way that brings credit to the Jewish people;

26. For the *mitzvah* we performed by accepting responsibility for the wrong we have committed, and not blaming our behavior on others;

27. For the *mitzvah* we performed by asking those whom we have hurt for forgiveness;

28. For the *mitzvah* we performed by not asking a storekeeper the price of an item when we had no intention of buying there;

29. For the *mitzvah* we performed by staying in close communication with our elderly parents;

30. For the *mitzvah* we performed by not serving liquor too generously at social events;

All these things God, please remember and inspire us to do more acts like these in the year ahead.

31. For the *mitzvah* we performed by not using words like "always" (e.g., "you're always inconsiderate") and "never" ("you never think before you act") when we are angry with someone;

32. For the *mitzvah* we performed by not making comments that can inflict irrevocable hurt on someone who has upset us;

33. For the *mitzvah* we performed by restricting our

expression of anger at someone to the incident that
provoked it;

34. For the *mitzvah* we performed by feeding our pets before
    eating ourselves;

35. For the *mitzvah* we performed by arranging to donate
    our organs for transplants;

36. For the *mitzvah* we performed by expressing gratitude on
    an ongoing basis to the people we are most likely to take
    for granted, our family members;

37. For the *mitzvah* we performed by helping someone in an
    unhappy frame of mind to laugh;

38. For the *mitzvah* we performed by treating our children
    and spouse with the same courtesy and kindness we
    extend to guests;

39. For the *mitzvah* we performed by donating the money
    we did not spend on food on Yom Kippur to a charity
    that feeds the poor;

40. For the *mitzvah* we performed when we were tempted to
    do something dishonest and refrained.

All these things God, please remember and inspire us to do
more acts like these in the year ahead.

This article is reprinted from A Code of Jewish Ethics (Volume 1) by Rabbi Joseph Telushkin, Crown Publishing , 2006, with permission from the author.

Yom Kippur

Rabbi Roly Matalon

Yom Kippur is about being immersed in spiritual work for an entire day. At some point, because of the fasting and the praying, there is a shift in your consciousness. You begin to approach and feel things differently. This allows you to be more sensitive and open.   You reach a heightened and productive spiritual state and then the door closes.

The liturgy uses the metaphor of the closing of the gates to symbolize the finite nature of life. You fast for an entire day; you have pushed yourself beyond what you thought was possible. Then the gate closes. So you have to get in as much as you can before then. Take advantage of being in that place, which is so productive spirituality, before the door closes. Push yourself beyond what you thought was possible. Do not miss that opportunity.

During Yom Kippur we are hungry. We could eat before the prescribed time, but we have to keep pushing ourselves. Too much prayer, too much fasting.–but we keep pushing ourselves. Spiritual life is forcing you or your self beyond your level of comfort and beyond your level of tolerance. That is what the High Holy Days ask us to do. Not all the time. There are moments of respite. There are moments of catching our breath. But we have to keep going.

A spiritual life is demanding, it is not some sort of instant nirvana. It requires work. Some people think that in a spiritual life you are just meditating and studying Torah. But really you are also going into the world and trying to change it. It is hard to see the things that we do not want to see. We have to push ourselves to be more and to do more.

Yom Kippur is giving us that message. If you push yourself, you will be able to do it. You will withstand it. If you push yourself, you can be great. It is about the greatness of the human being. It is the proof how great and spiritual we can be. The paradox of Yom Kippur is that at this moment of truth we are in the highest and lowest place   at the same time. In the moment of our highest spiritual elevation we are profoundly humbled by the deepest awareness of our failures, and at the same time, marveled at the amazing possibilities before us.

Reflection

Rabbi Roly Matalon

The Jewish Holy Days and Shabbat punctuate life. They give us an opportunity to think about different values, and issues. We can think about ourselves and our relationship with God, our community, and the world. We can try to enhance the different aspects of those relationships. Going through life without holidays and Shabbat is like reading a book without punctuation. You can't make sense of it.

My friend, Rabbi Irwin Kula, was speaking about the Jewish calendar as a spiritual technology. It is a tool that in itself doesn't have intrinsic meaning, but the holidays and Shabbat serve a purpose when we imbue them with meaning. They are the medium by which we are able to transform ourselves and the world. They help our world ascend into a place of greater holiness, *tikkun*, justice, peace. When we focus our spiritual energy on the theme of a particular holiday, the world has the potential to change accordingly. For example, Pesach is about freedom, coming out, leaving the narrow places. Shavuot is about the deep wisdom that is revealed to us each year. This is true for all the holy days.

Teshuva

David Solomon

The concept of *teshuva* has unfortunately become corrupted in our age. People think that *teshuva* is a decision that tomorrow I'm going to wake up and I'm going to be religious. I'm now going to keep *Shabbat*, keep *Kashrut*, put on *tefillin*, go to *shul*, and become a "*Baal Teshuva*," a religious person. That actually is a very corrupted form of *teshuva*. Those things, the performance of *mitzvot*, are what a Jew should be doing anyways. *Teshuva* is an inner transformation. *Teshuva* is the decision to act in a better way towards other people. The moment of *teshuva* begins when a person looks at themselves and says, "Why am I a rude person?" That is the beginning of *teshuva*.

We have one task in the world as a nation and that is to build a society based on social justice, preferably in the land of Israel. As individuals we have the task of rectifying creation as part of the movement of the universe towards its ultimate stage, which is a movement of *teshuva*. That can only begin with an inner transformation of the individual, a self awareness that allows us to act towards other people with authenticity, honesty, and dignity. *Teshuva* begins with my relationships with other people. Other then can that be used as a platform for my relationship with the Divine and the performance of *mitzvot*. We must, as a nation, fight against the things which brings into society disrepute. We must fight against corruption within ourselves. We must fight against oppression, exploitation, and the way people use each other on a daily basis. We must fight unhappiness in the world but we cannot do that until we fight the unhappiness within ourselves. Inner transformation is the beginning of *teshuva*. G-d and the prophets have assured us that teshuva is transformative. When I transform my inner self, I don't just transform myself, I transform the world around me. I become a beacon of light. It doesn't emanate from me alone, it emanates from G-d whose light comes through me as a conduit to the rest of the world. That is the true meaning of *teshuva*. To be a *kli* (vessel) for the light of G-d requires one to be self-reflective in the first instance and affect an inner transformation. That is the essence of *teshuva*.

Resolutions

Rabbi Roly Matalon

Resolutions are very individual. Every person has to work on their own issues. Some have to do with issues of anger, humility, arrogance, or confidence. These are human traits which are called *middot*. We work on our middot bur this work is complex. For example, sometimes I want to work on my anger, but I should be angry about certain things. I don't want to suppress my anger completely so where should I suppress it? Where is anger unproductive? Where do I deviate from my real goals and real connections with people? Where are the places that I should get angry? Anger is an important emotion because it moves us to do things. There are things we should be angry about in our world and in our lives. We have to make that discernment.

Then there are connections. Where am I connecting with my family? What do I need to repair? Where do I need to ask for forgiveness? Where have I been cruel? What commitments should I make for my intellectual and spiritual growth? What can I do to bring about justice in the world? What commitments will I make to protect the environment? There are so many ways prayer can guide us through these questions. There are materials which we superimpose on the prayer book and the holidays, resources that people have compiled, that help us categorize these things that we need to examine. They are some prayers that function like a kind checklist which some people find helpful. And we can't only think about questions in the synagogue. We need to think about them before, contemplate them during and remind ourselves of them after. Even when Yom Kippur is over, the gates have only metaphorically closed. There is still time to do *teshuva*; to think and rethink and then make resolutions to change. Monitoring your resolutions, throughout the year is crucial. Am I keeping true to my resolutions, to my word? It is very heavy this work, but it is life. Life is heavy. And if it not lived with that intensity and sense of purpose, then perhaps we are just wasting it.

At the End of Yom Kippur

Rabbi DovBer Pinson

Immediately following *Yom Kippur*, an entire day dedicated to forgiveness, we begin the traditional evening service, the Ma'ariv prayers, with the words, *V'Hu Rachum*… "And He, being merciful, will pardon iniquity…" What iniquity are we speaking of? We have just completed *Yom Kippur*, fasted, prayed, and reflected — now what? What iniquity could have possibly occurred in that short moment between the conclusion of *Yom Kippur* and the evening prayers? What Iniquities?

In that moment, between the conclusion of Yom Kippur and the evening service, there is just enough time to entertain one thought, and that could be, "Did it really work? Have I really been forgiven?" Having gone through the gut-wrenching, soul-bearing, body-transcending twenty-six hours of Yom Kippur, the greatest sin in the world would be to feel that maybe Yom Kippur was a waste, an empty gesture, maybe forgiveness was not granted. And so we say, *V'Hu Rachum, Hashem*, "O Merciful One, forgive us". Forgive us for thinking that we were not forgiven. Forgive us for being so down on ourselves, for being so doubtful.

The saddest and most devastating *kelipa*, "concealment", in the world, the greatest hindrance to any genuine spiritual growth is self-doubt and *yiush*, "despair", or giving up hope. A person cannot move forward with despair. There are those who doubt their abilities and then there are those who doubt themselves as people, sometimes because of past actions and sometimes maybe because of their upbringing or conditioning. To rid ourselves of this self-doubt and lack of belief in ourselves, and our future, we have to always remember that if G-d, the Master of the Universe, thinks that we are worth creating and sustaining at this very moment, then we are certainly worthy.

There is a point where you must move on. True, you need to deal with the past, but do not let it crowd out the present. There is no question that we need to fix what was wrong or broken, but it cannot take over your entire life. Sometimes we need to "stop" being in the past and begin focusing on the present and future, we need to let go of the "imperfect self" and begin focusing on the now, on the eternal and "perfect self." When we fall we should never give up hope and begin feeling that we are a failure. We need to get back up and learn to cut our losses, at least for the time being, in order to move on.

To be forgiven means to be released from the weight of your past actions. When your negative past no longer blocks entry to the gift of the present, you can be sure that you have been forgiven. This can occur in a tangible way, or even in a psychological fashion. Not to say that you relinquish ownership of those past actions, or that you simply throw them away, but that you acknowledge those actions as "my problems", while at the same time acknowledging that, "I am forgiven. I can live freely in the moment, I can be here now". Happy New Year!

Rabbi DovBer Pinson

Rav DovBer Pinson is a world-renowned rabbi, prolific author, and kabbalists, recognized as one of the world's foremost authorities on authentic Kabbalah and Judaic philosophy. He is a beloved spiritual teacher and a mentor to many. Through his books, lectures, seminars and consul he has touched and inspired the lives of tens of thousands the world over.

Among his published works are;

Reincarnation & Judaism; The Journey of the Soul

Inner Rhythms; The Kabbalah of Music

Meditation & Judaism; Jewish Meditative Paths

Toward the Infinite

Jewish Wisdom on the Afterlife: The Mysteries, the Myths, & the Meanings

Upsherin; A Boys First Hair Cut

Tefilin: A Guide & Deeper Exploration of Tefilin

Thirty-Two Gates of Wisdom; Awakening through Kabbalah

Eight Lights; 8 Meditations for Chanukah

The Purim Reader: The Holiday of Purim Explored

The IYYUN Hagadah: The Hagadah Companion

Reclaiming the Self: The Way of Teshuvah:

Rav DovBer Pinson is the Rosh Yeshiva of the IYYUN Yeshiva and heads IYYUN Center in Brownstone Brooklyn (www. IYYUN.com).

Rabbi Joseph Telushkin

Joseph Telushkin, named by *Talk* Magazine as one of the 50 best speakers in the United States, is the author of *Jewish Literacy: The Most Important Things to Know About the Jewish Religion, Its People and Its History.* The most widely selling book on Judaism of the past two decades, *Jewish Literacy* has been hailed by leading figures in all the major movements of Judaism, and has been published in a third edition (June, 2008).

In 2006, Bell Tower/Crown published the first volume of his monumental work, *A Code of Jewish Ethics: You Shall be Holy,* a comprehensive presentation of Jewish teachings on the vital topic of personal character and integrity. Richard Joel, president of Yeshiva University, called the book, "a gift to humankind," and Rabbi David Wolpe hailed it "as a remarkable guide to goodness." In 2007, *A Code of Jewish Ethics* won the National Jewish Book Award as the Jewish book of the year. Volume 2 of the Code, subtitled, "Love Your Neighbor as Yourself" was published in 2009 to great acclaim.

In September, 2010, Telushkin published *Hillel: If Not Now, When?* A biography of the great talmudic sage which makes

the argument as to why Hillel should emerge as the great
rabbinic figure of the 21st century. The book discussed
in detail Hillel's open and encouraging attitude to non-
Jews interested in Judaism and in converting. Telushkin
is currently writing a study of the life and impact of the
Lubavitcher Rebbe.

Rabbi Telushkin's earlier book, *Words that Hurt, Words that
Heal* became the motivating force behind Senators Joseph
Lieberman and Connie Mack's 1996 Senate Resolution # 151
to establish a "National Speak No Evil Day" throughout the
United States.

He has also written *Jewish Humor: What the Best Jewish
Jokes Say About the Jews.* Larry Gelbart, author of *Mash*
and *Tootsie* said that "I don't know if Jews are really the
chosen people, but I think Joseph Telushkin's book makes a
strong argument that we're the funniest." Telushkin is also
co-author with Dennis Prager of one of the most influential
Jewish books published in the last thirty-five years, *The Nine
Questions People Ask About Judaism,* hailed by Herman
Wouk as "the intelligent skeptic's guide to Judaism."

In 1997, his novel, *An Eye for an Eye,* became the basis
for four episodes of David Kelley's Emmy Award-winning
ABC TV series, *The Practice,* and he co-write (with Allen
Estrin) three additional episodes of the program. Telushkin
was the co-writer with David Brandes and the Associate
Producer of the 1991 film, *The Quarrel.* The film, an
American Playhouse production, and the winner of the Santa

Barbara Film Festival, was released theatrically throughout the United States.

Rabbi Telushkin was ordained at Yeshiva University in New York, and pursued graduate studies in Jewish history at Columbia University. He resides in New York City with his wife, Dvorah Menashe Telushkin, and they have four children.

Telushkin lectures throughout the United States, serves as a Senior Associate of CLAL, and on the Board of Directors of the Jewish Book Council.

Rabbi Roly Matalon

Rabbi J. Rolando Matalon came to B'nai Jeshurun in 1986 to share the pulpit with his mentor and friend Rabbi Marshall T. Meyer. Together they transformed this small, declining synagogue into a revitalized congregation (that today has a membership of more than 1,800 households) committed to an inclusive approach to liturgy and community and dedicated to the work of education, social justice, and interfaith cooperation.

Following the untimely death of Rabbi Meyer in 1993, Rabbi Matalon assumed BJ's rabbinic leadership; in 1995 Rabbi Marcelo Bronstein—another student of Rabbi Meyer—joined him in rabbinic partnership, and in 2001 Rabbi Felicia L. Sol became the third member of the spiritual leadership of the congregation.

Rabbi Matalon serves on the boards of a number of agencies and organizations including American Friends of Parents Circle, the International Advisory Board of the International Center for Interfaith Dialogue (Doha, Qatar), Beit Tefillah Israeli-Tel Aviv, the President's Advisory Council of Union Theological Seminary, Habitat for Humanity's Leadership Council, and the Advisory Board of Storahtelling. Rabbi

Matalon has received awards from the New York Board of Rabbis, the Jewish Peace Fellowship, and the New Israel Fund.

José Rolando Matalon was born in Buenos Aires, Argentina, in 1956. He attended the Universidad de Buenos Aires and the Université de Montreal, where he received a B.S. in chemistry. He went on to study at the Seminario Rabinico Latinoamericano in Buenos Aires, with his teacher Rabbi Meyer, and attended the Hebrew University of Jerusalem for one year. In 1982 he came to New York to complete his studies for the rabbinate at the Jewish Theological Seminary of America, and he received his ordination and Master of Hebrew Letters there in 1986.

Rabbi Matalon is a founding co-director of Piyut North America, a partnership between B'nai Jeshurun and Hazmanah Le-Piyut in Israel. He plays the 'ud (Arabic lute) and is a member of the New York Arabic Orchestra. Rabbi Matalon is married and has two daughters.

David Solomon

David Solomon is an internationally recognized scholar, translator, teacher and writer across a range of disciplines. David has taught extensively at all levels of education, from primary school to adult education in a range of subjects, and is regarded by many as one of the most gifted and inspiring teachers they have encountered. He is perhaps best known throughout much of the Jewish world today for his dynamic 'In One Hour' overview talks and for his in-depth lectures on Jewish History, Tanach, Jewish Philosophy, Hebrew and Kabbalah.

David is an experienced translator of an extensive range of classical Kabbalistic texts and scholarly monographs. He is currently based in Sydney as Neshama Life's Scholar-in-Residence, where he is working on the first-ever English translation of the kabbalistic text Tiqunei HaZohar.

Australian born, David has studied in several yeshivot in Australia and Israel, and has degrees in English Literature, Anthropology, Media and Jewish Studies (and has taught and written extensively on Conceptual Art).

For more information or to listen to an extensive collection of David's freely available lectures visit www.inonehour.net.

About Sinai Live Books

Sinai Live is committed to assisting high-quality teachers share their wisdom. Our goal is to enhance our readers' personal Jewish journeys and elevate everyday life through thoughtful and insightful content. We aim to engage, inspire and encourage further exploration.

Our books include:

Telushkinisms: Wisdom to the Point
by Rabbi Joseph Telushkin

Footsteps: Perspectives for Daily Life
by Rebbetzin Esther Jungreis

Insights: Concise and Thoughtful Jewish Wisdom
by Rabbi Benjamin Blech

More Precious Than Pearls: A Prayer for the Women of Valor in Our Lives
edited by Mark B. Pearlman

Passport to Kabbalah: A Journey of Inner Transformation
by Rabbi DovBer Pinson

The World from a Spiritual Perspective: A Collection of Insightful Essays from Aish.com
by Rabbi Benjamin Blech

Visit www.sinailive.com or contact us at info@sinailive.com to learn more.

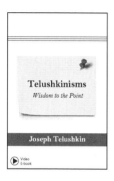

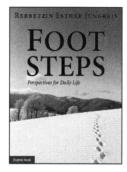

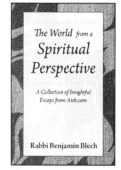

About Rethink Partners

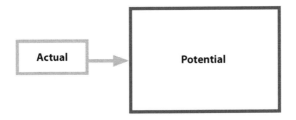

This reading experience was developed by Mark Pearlman's Rethink Partners, an organization dedicated to shifting user and industry perspectives through a combination of business strategy, product management, sales and marketing, editorial, design and online implementation.

Rethink Partners works with for-profit and non-profit organizations to help them reach their potential. We are focused on seeing both what is and what could be.

Visit us at www.rethinkpartners.com.

Acknowledgements

This book would not have been possible without the help of many people. Special thanks goes to:

Marc Suvall, a member of the Sinai Live advisory board, for his content advice and editorial assistance.

Jake Laub, for his creativity in design and diligence in editing.

Raquel Amram, for her meticulous transcriptions and editing.

Daniel Schanler, for his expertise in video editing and production.